EMOTION POO

Don't Let It Stick to You!

Don't look at me, I don't know what she's on about.

Written by
Lainy Wills

Illustrated by
Espen Meling Sele

AuthorHouse™ UK
1663 Liberty Drive
Bloomington, IN 47403 USA
www.authorhouse.co.uk
Phone: 0800.197.4150

Published by AuthorHouse 10/29/2015

ISBN: 978-1-5049-9090-5 (sc)
ISBN: 978-1-5049-9089-9 (e)

Library of Congress Control Number: 2015917507

Print information available on the last page.

Any people depicted in stock imagery provided by Thinkstock are models,
and such images are being used for illustrative purposes only.
Certain stock imagery © Thinkstock.

This book is printed on acid-free paper.

authorHOUSE®

I dedicate this book to all students, past, present, and future, of Phoenix Therapies and Training. They inspire me to feel brave enough to share my ideas and to follow my emotional-poo-destroying dreams.

Acknowledgements

Thanks to my lovely partner, Kev, and our daughter, Scarlett, whom I love endlessly. They also give me loads of practice using my poo alarm and shield, and let me throw my emotional poo at them – for research purposes only, of course.

Thanks to my friends Angela Reece Davis, Caroline Sutton, Kim Evans Johns, Alison Philips James, and Jeanette for letting me delve around in their emotional poo. Huge thanks to Suzi Morris and Tim Lawler for editing my shockingly bad English. I must have been off sick when spelling and grammar were taught at school. Thank you to Nadia Morris (the best god-daughter ever), Dan Morris, and Evie Morris for checking to make sure that the book wasn't too pooey.

Thanks to Espen, the artist who made the poo character so very real. The research he engaged in to do this led him to some weird and wonderful places. I don't think he will ever forgive me. Thanks to Nina Sele for introducing me to her amazingly talented nephew.

Thank you to Paula North, my business partner and friend, who helps me to escape the poo when it does get me.

I want to thank Angela Reece Davis twice because once just isn't enough for all the constant support that she gives to me.

Hello, and thanks for pooping in. This book is going to show you how to stop yourself from getting upset when people are mean to you. We are going to call other people's meanness "emotional poo." Why?

Don't look at me,
I don't know
what she's
on about.

Would you pick up someone else's poo with your bare hands?

Aargh! Of course not.

Well, people's mean words are their emotional poo.

We don't pick up people's physical poo, so let's not pick up their emotional poo either.

So where does emotional poo come from?

It comes from people who feel one, two, or all three of the following feelings:

- Mad

- Bad

- Sad

You're probably thinking by now that you are the only nice person in the whole wide world.

Wrong.

Guess what you do when you feel mad, bad, or sad?

Yep, you guessed it – you throw *your* emotional poo around.

What does emotional poo look like?

It comes in many shapes and sizes, but it all *stinks!*

you're fat...

you're stupid

no-one loves you

you are a
waste of
space

you're a prat

you
always
get it
wrong

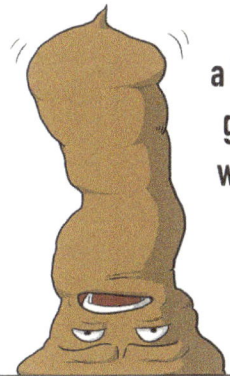

So what do we do with it?

We carry it around with us all day, every day.

Why? Because we don't realise that that's what we are doing.

But we do realise it now. Oh yeah.

So how do we get rid of this emotional poo?

With the most powerful things in the world: our minds.

Your mind has the power to create and destroy, so let's use it to destroy your emotional poo.

You can clean away your emotional poo in seven ways, as follows:

1. Write a list of all the mean things that people have said to you and that you believe.

2. Either draw a picture of a big piece of poo or else buy a plastic piece of poo from a joke shop. Wrap the list around the poo and stick it on with tape so it can't come off. Then get rid of it.

You can throw it in the bin,

bury it somewhere far away,

throw it into the sea,

or burn it (with an adult's supervision, of course).

This is the beginning of your mind starting to let go of the poo.

3. Know what you are good at.

We are all diamonds, beautiful and shiny.

We all have special qualities. Find out what yours are. Write a new list of what you are good at. What are your strengths? Ask your parents, teachers, and friends, and the other kind people around you.

Read your list every time you feel mad, bad, or sad.

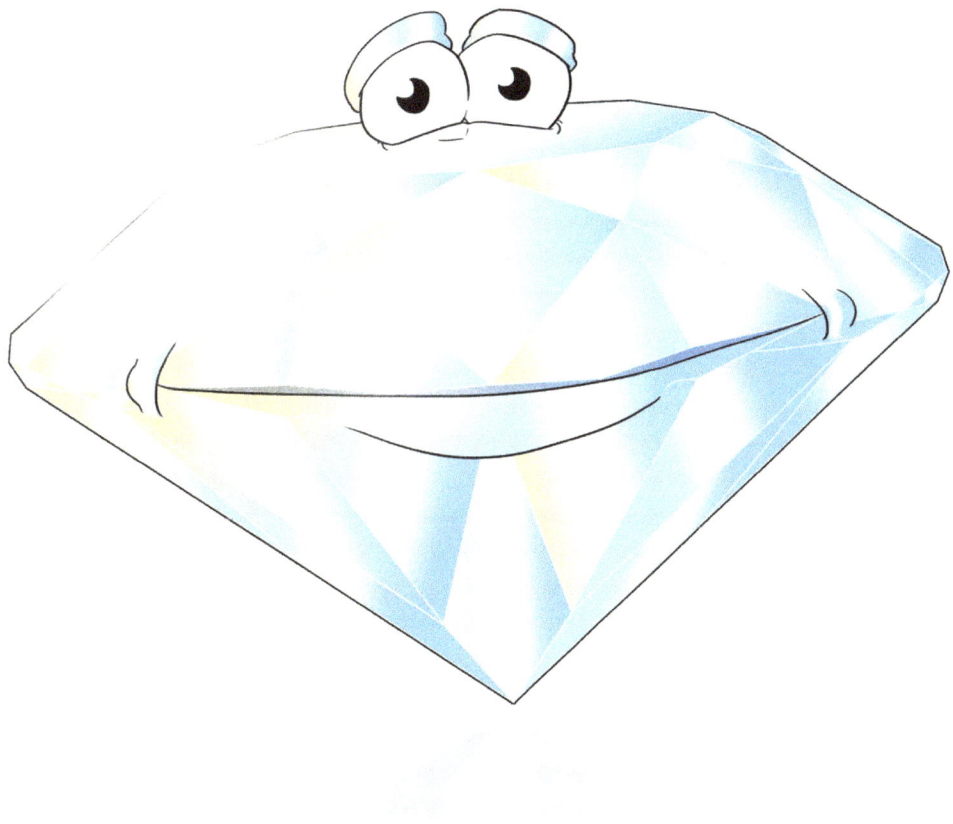

4. Learn to be calm.

Being calm makes your emotional poo go away.

When we are mad, bad, or sad, we can better see our emotional poo.

Being calm is like a magic wand. *Poof*– the emotional poo is gone.

Become calm by taking big, deep breaths, pushing your tummy out as much as you can when you inhale.

YouTube is a place where you can find videos showing millions of relaxation exercises. These are called meditations.

Meditating is like washing your mind. It stops your thoughts from stinking.

Breath in...
And out...
Yes...
Now, relax...

breath in...

5. Think about what you can be happy about.

What's nice about your life?

Whom do you like?

Who likes you?

What do you enjoy doing?

What are you good at?

What fun have you had?

Think about what is good in your life, not what is bad.

I love travelling

I love walks in the forest

I love film

I love
my country

I love cheese

... And I
LOVE
my cat!

I love my friends

I love dancing

I love th

I love my family

I love chocolate

I love making food

I love my hair

e danger

I love my drawing tablet

6. You can use your body to help you to feel brave.

Try this: Stand with your arms up in the air. Imagine roots growing from your feet. Smile as much as you can whilst you look up into the sky for two minutes.

See how it makes you feel.

This posture is called the power stance. Do you see why?

To make this extra-powerful, you can assume the power stance as you look into a mirror and remind yourself of your strengths.

THE POWER STANCE

The previous six techniques showed you how to get rid of emotional poo. How can you stop from collecting more of it?

Easy.

7. Use an emotional poo alarm!

When anyone is mean to you, imagine an alarm going off in your head. Ask the person kindly, "Are you feeling mad, bad, or sad? Take some deep breaths; you will feel better."

Now you know how to protect yourself from other people's mean words.

Have fun sharing these techniques with your friends so that they can protect themselves too.

Look out for more books to teach you how to deal with feeling mad, bad, and sad.

MAD BAD SAD

This is not just a fun book to read; it is also a fun book to follow. Why? Because it shows you how to use seven keys to happiness to destroy emotional poo. Doing so will make you feel safer, calmer, and happier. Like all keys, though, they work only if you use them. If you do not believe that they will work for you, just try them.

These seven keys have already been tried and tested by me, my family, some of my friends, and hundreds of my students. I wrote this book because they told me to share these keys, especially with children, so that other people could prevent the build-up of emotional poo.

If you want to become an official "emotional poo destroyer," please write to me. I will send you an emotional poo alarm and a certificate. And stay tuned for my forthcoming follow-up book, *How to Deal with Feeling Mad, Bad, and Sad.*

Bye for now.

About the Author

Lainy Wills, 47⅞ years old, lives in Leicester with her partner, Kev, and their daughter, Scarlett, aka Loolaa. Lainy loves destroying emotional poo. It is her job, her hobby, and her passion. In fact, you could say it's her mission. She is an "emotional poo destroyer."

What is emotional poo? Well, it's the name for the mean things that people say to us and that we decide to believe are true; for example, "You are stupid."

"Why is Lainy so committed to destroying emotional poo?" people ask. Well, because she spent nearly thirty years living in a massive emotional poo pit. Then one day she got fed up and said, "There must be more to life than this." So she went on an adventure to discover how to escape the emotional poo pit and be happier.

On this adventure, she found seven simple, fun, powerful ways to be free and to create a new life. Now she wants to share these ways with everyone so that they can be free and happier too.

Do you want to be an emotional poo warrior? If you do, you can join Lainy's gang and get a certificate and your destroyer kit. Lainy is very nosy, so she would love to hear your stories about your adventure out of the poo pit too. Please share them with her. Thanks – and enjoy.

About the Book

This book helps children and parents to take a fun look at solving serious problems, for example being bullied, feeling stressed, and feeling hurt. It offers practical, powerful, simple, and fun solutions to all these troubles.

"Emotional poo" is a concept the author has created to represent the mean things that people say to others. She invites her readers to treat other people's mean comments as if they were pieces of poo. What would you do if someone tried to give you a piece of poo?

This book uses children's strengths to their full advantage and allows children to pick and choose how they do this. The book also offers seven different keys to protect children, each of which involves powerful games that teach children how to feel emotionally stronger and safer.

This is not just a book to read and laugh at; it's a book to use. It contains powerful lessons that can be used every day over and over again to keep you feeling happier. Like all keys, though, they work only if you use them. If you do not believe that they will work for you, just try them.

The suggestions in this book are like sweets: you will like some and not others, and your friends will like different ones than you do. That's OK. We are all different.

If you learn other ways to get rid of the poo, please let me know, as I am still learning too.

Thanks – and enjoy.

Lightning Source UK Ltd.
Milton Keynes UK
UKHW051329081221
395296UK00005B/17

9 781504 990905